MY STRONG MIND
III

I SET GOALS AND WORK HARD TO DELIVER THEM

by **NIELS VAN HOVE**

Published in Australia by Truebridges Media

First published in Australia 2020
Copyright © Niels van Hove 2020
All rights reserved. No part of this publication may be reproduced, stored in a retrieval system, or transmitted, in any form or by any means without the prior written permission of the publisher, nor be otherwise circulated in any form of binding or cover other than that in which it is published and without a similar condition being imposed on the subsequent purchaser.

National Library of Australia Cataloguing-in-Publication entry
Creator: Van Hove, Niels
Title: My Strong Mind: I Set Goals and Work Hard to Deliver Them
e-book: 978-0-6485641-2-6
KPD paperback: 978-0-6485641-3-3
Ingram paperback: 978-0-6485641-4-0
Ingram hardback: 978-0-6485641-5-7

Target Audience: For primary school age
Subjects: Juvenile fiction. Confidence in children. Self-esteem. Toughness (personal trait).

Cover layout and illustrations by Vanlaldiki
Typesetting by Nelly Murariu (PixBeeDesign.com)
Printed by Kindle Direct Publishing & Ingramspark

Disclaimer
All care has been taken in the preparation of the information herein, but no responsibility can be accepted by the publisher or author for any damages resulting from the misinterpretation of this work. All contact details given in this book were current at the time of publication, but are subject to change.

Jack and Kate are good **friends**. They enjoy learning and playing together.

At school, they **learned** about how to improve their strong mind.

Their teacher taught them that you can use your strong mind to improve **COMMITMENT**. **COMMITMENT** means that you set your own goals and work hard to deliver them.

A goal can be **anything** you want to achieve in the future. Be it tomorrow, next week or next year.

When you **set a goal** and reach it, you feel satisfied and proud of yourself.

Kate and Jack realised that **reaching** their goals is not always easy.

- Reaching a goal often takes **time** and **practise**.
- It is hard to stay **focused** on one task.
- You can feel **upset** or **angry** and want to give up.

They wanted to share everything they learned just with you!

- ☑ Get dressed
- ☑ Brush teeth
- ☑ Brush hair
- ☑ Pack bag
- ☑ Pack lunch

I used to be **slow** to get ready for school.

Then I made a **list of tasks** to follow every morning to get ready in time.

Now, when I tick off my last task in the morning, I feel very **proud** of myself.

My **daily routine** made reaching my morning goal much easier.

I sometimes found it hard to concentrate whilst reading.

Then I set a time goal to read without distraction.

First for **two minutes...**

then **five...**

then **ten!**

Now, when the alarm rings after ten minutes of reading, I feel good about myself.

I **improved** my reading stamina with a time goal.

'I'm not giving up'
or
'go for it, Kate!'

This helped me to focus and keep trying.

This is how I learned to do cartwheels.

Positive self-talk helped me to reach my goal.

This is how I **practised** in front of a large crowd. Safely, in my own mind.

Now, I love playing in front of my class. **Imagination** helped me to reach my goal.

Some goals are **not exciting**. You don't want to work on them, but you must.

We never liked practising our timetables. Then we made up a game.

We would throw two dice.

The first one of us to **multiply** both numbers shown on the dice and say the outcome, won the game.

Making a game out of a goal we didn't like, made it **more fun.**

Sometimes our goals are so **complicated**, we get stuck and want to give up.

Like when we were building a big Lego house or an electronic robot.

We would imagine a motivation ladder.
And go **up... up... up!** One step at a time.

The **motivation ladder** helped us to keep working toward our goal.

When I'm **struggling** to play a new song, I sometimes get frustrated, upset, or angry.

I feel like screaming and giving up.

When that happens, I lie down and take five *ginormous* breaths.

1...2...3...4...5

Breathing calms me down and gets me ready to try and reach my goal.

Sometimes my parents make me commit to a goal.

Boring **chores** like cleaning my room, setting the table or doing the dishes.

My mum says:

'That's just life, Kate. Sometimes you have to commit to goals you don't like.'

Kate and Jack try to set their own goals and work hard to deliver them.

This is how they improve their commitment.

Showing commitment is hard, but Jack and Kate do not easily give up.

Every time they try, their **minds grow** just a little bit **stronger**.

MY STRONG MIND III

Commitment

My name is _____
and I set goals and work hard to deliver them.

My SMARTER goal

Specific: What exactly am I going to do?
_____
_____

Measureable: How do I know I reached my goal?
_____
_____

Actions: What steps can I take to reach my goal?
_____
_____

Realistic: How difficult do I think this goal is?

1   2   3   4   5

Easy   Very hard

Timeliness: When should I reach my goal?

_____

_____

Excitement: How much do I like this goal?

NOTES FOR PARENTS

What is Mental Toughness?

Mental Toughness* is a combination of resilience, the curiosity and drive to grow yourself, and confidence in your own abilities and interactions with people. Mental Toughness has been used in elite sport psychology for many years to increase performance, and it applies to everyday life too.

There are four attributes that characterise Mental Toughness, also called The Four Cs:

Commitment: I set goals and work hard to deliver them.

Control: I'm pro-active and keep my emotions in check.

Challenge: I stretch myself and learn from everything.

Confidence: I have the ability and can stand my ground.

Research shows that mentally tough children perform up to 25% better in exams. They sleep better, are more engaged in the classroom, and have higher aspirations. They also transition more successfully from junior to secondary education, perceive less bullying, and are less likely to adopt anti-social behaviour.

The commitment attribute of mental toughness describes the extent to which someone is prepared to set goals and make measurable promises that, once made, they will work hard to deliver on. We can be sure our children will have to deal with adversity and need to show commitment during their life. The examples in this book simply show some techniques and small interventions that can lead to increased commitment and better outcomes.

---

* Refers to *Developing Mental Toughness: Improving Performance, Wellbeing and Positive Behaviours in Others* by Peter Clough and Doug Strycharczyk.

ABOUT THE AUTHOR

Niels is a father of two girls and lives with his wife in Melbourne, Australia. He is an author and mental toughness advocate. With his books, he hopes to make a positive difference, promote conversation, and help children learn about confidence, resilience, and a positive mindset.

Other books in the *My Strong Mind* series

ABOUT THE ILLUSTRATOR

Vanlaldiki is a digital artist and an illustrator from Mizoram, India. She fell in love with drawing when her dad drew his idea of their new home with colourful sketch-pens. She is a self-taught artist with 8 years experience and has worked with clients all over the world.

Go to **www.mentaltoughness.online** to download a free mental toughness e-book for adults or fun exercises to do with your kids at home. For teachers, I provide over twenty-five exercises to use at school.

Ingram Content Group UK Ltd.
Milton Keynes UK
UKHW050401200623
423718UK00002B/22